For Updates Follow:
Instagram.com/AntonioILiranzo
Twitter.com/AntonioILiranzo
AntonioLiranzo.com

First Printing, 2021

Front & Back Cover: Richard Bohan
Inside Planet Art: Michelle Riofrio
Editors: Viterbo Liranzo, Samuel Rider, Audrey Brown

Acknowledgments

I can't believe this is my third book in less than a year! Thank you to everyone who has supported me and purchased a copy of my last two books. I truly appreciate all the support and love! I have experienced a lot in this life and wanted to create a book that allowed me to talk about the process of becoming the person I am destined to be. I hope you all can relate to the messages in this book. Of course, this book couldn't have been created without the help of an amazing team:

To my editors: First and foremost, my bestie and brother, Viterbo Liranzo, this is our third book working together, it truly is amazing to have you alongside this journey to space! You helped me realize some things last year that really started my transformation, thank you! Second, my good friend, Samuel Rider. Thank you so much for helping me edit. This is our second book we have worked on together and it means so much to me. I was able to share my knowledge of astrology with you and this has been an amazing experience to be able to work together. Third, my good friend, Audrey Brown. I love that this has been our second book together! I love having you on this journey with me, you are my crystal sister, we talk about planet alignments, self growth, and metaphysical properties

Antonio's Return

ANTONIO LIRANZO

Antonio Liranzo

Other Books By Antonio Liranzo

Falling Angel: Rising Phoenix (2020)
Romance In A Modern World (2021)

all the time. This just feels like the right book to work with you on, thank you!

Shoutout to my artists that worked with me, Richard Bohan,this is our second book working together and I love how your art brings my vision to life. The cover and the back cover came out so beautiful! Thank you for always collaborating with me! My second artist, Michelle Riofrio, the details in your sketches on the inside are beautiful! Your work for my last book, *Romance In A Modern World*, was amazing, I am so happy to be working with you on my latest creation.

Enjoy the ride of life and the universe. Aside from 2020 being a crazy year, I was thrown a lot of challenges, but I was able to use my writing as a way to combat these obstacles. I am so happy to share this work with you all! Thank you!

Preface

For the past few years I have experienced a great amount of change. As they say, it takes Saturn 29.5 years to revolve around the sun. Astrologist believe that this marks our Saturn Return. I can attest to that and say in the past two years of my life, I have seen immense change happening. I wanted to write a book based on the themes of Astrology and the planet's meaning. As a big believer in the universe and manifestation, it has become part of my daily spiritual practice. In my previous books, I have shared a lot about my mental health and romantic life. Now it's time to share the journey of learning about the man that I am destined to become! Writing this book has been amazingly therapeutic for me and I hope I covered topics that can help every reader. These topics are split into several parts by the meaning of each planet/star. I hope you are ready for a ride into space.

Contents

6
MARS (SEX & ACTION)

7
JUPITER (ABUNDANCE & GROWTH)

The universe has your back!

ANTONIO'S RETURN

1

The Sun (Personality & Vitality)

Let me warm you up
Planets revolve around the sun
Can we revolve around love?

The source of heat and energy
You know humans have kinetic energy
Why don't we set a spark?

When we cuddle
Your body temperature makes me so warm
On this cold February night.

The sun is almost a perfect sphere
See, even the sun has its flaws
It's ok if we don't always see eye to eye.

It's time you let me brighten your galaxy.

10.20

10.20.1991
A sensitive Libra was born
An Italian, first generation, new mother held her
son close to her heart
She didn't know this is what she needed to restart
her life.

She named her newborn son, Antonio
Her father, died on 10.20
This rebirth woke something that was dead in her
for a while.
The universe was giving her a purpose again.

This 10.20 baby turned into a teenager
He went through a lot of trauma
A bad relationship with his dad
Was homeless twice
But never lost his optimism.

As Antonio became a young adult

Sexuality exploration became prominent
It was time that he took his life into his own hands
Experimenting and learning about himself through
his LGBTQ+ friends.

Antonio decided to head to the big city of dreams
10.20 kept showing up every time he would check
his phone or watch
It is a number that reminds you that your angel is
watching you and you will have obstacles along the
way, but you will overcome them and grow on your
journey.

As Antonio approached his thirties
He looked back at all his dreams
Where his grandpa, Antonio, would visit him
It all clicked, 10.20 is a cosmic combination of a
past life (Antonio) sparking new life into (The Mother)
from her newborn (Antonio) sharing the same time-
line.

Call it a coincidence
He called it a universal experience
The cosmic attachment he has to this date is so
empowering
10.20 is more than a birthday
It's a day that brought back life into his mother!

Even as a newborn, he knew his role was to heal
and bring joy <3.

Libra Tingz

Yes, I am indecisive as fuck
Trust me, my brother gets so annoyed when I call
him to ask what shirt to wear
· Yea, I am a hopeless romantic
I may dive in way too deep after date three.

Being love drunk all the time
Gives the worst hangover
I thrive in social settings, let's hang!
Having a fling with someone has become my new
obsession.

I love when people are open minded
Let's all love and embrace each other
Being diplomatic and fair
Let's keep the peace and see both sides of this de-
bate.

I try to see the best in people
I have learned how to listen to my intuition

I will give everyone a fair chance
But once I am taken advantage of, it's time for this
air sign to fly away!

If you can handle all these sides to me, then let's
take a journey around space.

Alive

Oh, I've arrived
Do you feel my presence?
You know what that is?
Good energy.

I am here to be me
I am here to help the world go round
I am here to live
I am here to redefine what it means to be a human.

I feel good
Getting high off of...
Love and life
My vision is finally so clear.

20/20
Hell of a year
Rings of saturn had me spinning in circles
But I never got lost in this whirlwind.

Had some epiphanies
Rising phoenix visions
Avoided some black holes in my life
Are you ready to feel my power?

Lunar + Solar Eclipse

An amazing phenomenon
Be my eclipse?
One celestial body covering the other
When I have dark moments, will you be my light?

I am looking for when two become one
I don't want codependency
I want a partner that will support me
Cover me how the Earth's shadow covers the
moon.

Protect my light from being dimmed by the outside
world
The observer just sees a source of light being cov-
ered
What they don't see
Is the magic we have in our galaxy!

I am your solar and you are my lunar eclipse.

Milky Way

Floating among the stars
Can you be my milky way?
Like the chocolate bar
Sweet and juicy on the inside
With one bite, you leak out...

Let me enter your galaxy
There are about 125 billion out there
But you are the most important one
Let me be the sun that keeps you warm...

Can You Feel It?

This realm
As if we traveled through time
I can't explain this blissful moment.

It's a rebirth
A new chapter
A spark
A miracle.

Shooting stars everywhere
So many planets in orbit
Cosmic sensation
Is this how it feels to finally understand myself?

Venus be my strength of love
Saturn guide me to a new beginning
Jupiter show me luck and wealth
Sun show me what vitality is.

Let's not speak

Just hold my hand
Feel my energy and what it means
We can travel to the end of time together.

Can you feel it?

2

Mercury (Communication & Intellect)

Like a phoenix rising from the sun
I learned that I don't want to talk about the surface
level
My will is strong and I want to discover what is hid-
den, the unseen power
This timing feels right, to express myself.

My inner awareness and empathy powers are growing
My lust for life is real
I am an acute observer
Silence is powerful.

Mercury is the planet of communication and intellect
Mine happens to be in Scorpio
My view on life is very different
I see the world with intuition.

I speak with my body
I may seem harsh
But I prefer getting straight to the matter
I can be intense, serious, and a bit obsessive.

I never said hanging with me was easy
The intensity is at an all time high
I refuse to limit myself for anyone, anymore.
This journey just started.

I have been through a lot in 29.5 years
It's time to process everything
My wings are spread and I am going to keep on flying
The universe will show me who I am supposed to be.

The Frog Or The Prince?

You always read about
The princess kissing the frog
This magical kiss turns the frog
Into a prince...

I have to laugh at this fairytale ending
We all know I have a wounded heart
The "princes" I have fell in and out of love with
Have left me stranded in a dark swamp.

Drowning in a swamp of my tears
I would prefer the prince to stay, a frog
These "princes" with horrible communication skills
I would prefer talking to a frog.

After you've dated all the "princes" in the kingdom
You start building a shield for your love

There are a lot of men that will claim to be your
prince charming
I use my imagination and turn them into a frog.

It's easier to walk away from an animal that can't
talk
Than a man that will try to use persuasion
To trap you in their
Fairytale love game!

Vulnerability

If I told you that I will never lie
If I told you that I will lay my heart right here on
the floor
If I told you that I would take a bullet for you
Would you stay or leave?

If I showed you my demons
If I showed you my weakness
If I showed you my tears
Would you stay or leave?

If I felt hurt
If I felt sad
If I felt lost
Would you stay or leave?

If I told you I love being vulnerable
Would you stay or leave?

Addicted To The Chase

I can't be attached
Yet
I seem to be
Hooked.

I believe, humans in society
Are taught that love should be a game
To chase and have someone hooked
I am too sensitive for this shit!

Yet, I am here waiting for your texts
I have a good read on people
I already know you will leave me on read for the
next two hours
Knowing this, I am still choosing to be blind to the
matter.

Why can't we openly tell each other
That we like each other
I have a crush on you
Let's see if you want to make me yours.

I get it
The high
Of being
Addicted to the chase.

One day though
We both will be out of breath
I will need my lungs to be filled
I won't be breathing you, but instead, someone
else...

You were so addicted to the chase
That you ran past your chance
And that chance was...
Me!

Materialism Is Overrated

I don't do that superficial shit
You can't buy me with money
Flashy things are nice in the moment
Shiny toys lose their shine after awhile.

If you want me to stick around
Let's talk about life
Let's get deep
Let's support each other on an authentic level.

I don't work to make money
I do what I love for a living
I used to fall in the trap thinking that I need flashy
things to satisfy my needs
I am finally awake.

My self worth

Does not depend on my net worth
To make my life work
I dive deeper into myself
To see what my heart is worth.

So Nice

That feeling when a first date goes well
A deep conversation
We forget the superficial shit
We dive into what feels right.

The energy being exchanged across the table
Looking into your eyes makes me feel so seen
Vulnerability is my playing card
You are the dealer.

Let's not cut this date short
This conversation is so amazing
We grab more drinks
Talk about our goals and what legacy we want to
leave on this earth.

People say that sex on the first date is bad
But, this energy is too incredible to ignore
We have a magical night

My lips on your lips
Your hand on my ****.

The next morning
The feeling of amazement is still there
Waking me up to intense cuddles
I love this pure feeling!
This interaction has given me new hope in love and
dating.

It feels so nice...

3

Venus (Love & Harmony)

Love
Like my ruling planet
Let me take you to...
VENUS!

I am a true romantic at heart
I thrive in committed relationships
Ruler of love
Don't break my heart.

One of my favorite paintings
Birth Of Venus
The vulnerability Aphorditie has
Is so empowering!

My Venus is in Pisces
I yearn for a deep connection with someone
I use to not believe in having boundaries with love
I will forgive, but I will remain aware when my energy
is being taken advantage of!

Venus, bring me your cosmic energy
I am ready for love
I understand compassion now
I understand self-love now.

Maybe I can be someone's aphrodisiac one day...
I am open to a connection with another vulnerable
heart.

Show Me Love
And Light

Words of affirmation with your tongue ties
So excited
To tell me
You love me.

Always surprising me
Everyday with you feels likes Christmas
Little surprises when you come to the door
Your love is a gift.

Stressed out
I have so much work to get done
You jump in and help
Love your acts of service.

You know I love the bedroom
Your touch soothes my soul
Knowing how to calm down my body

Physical touch sending chills down my spine.

The biggest love sign for me is
Your time
Quality time
Happens every time I am with you.

We have multiple love languages
Love is a spectrum
We aren't in a box
Love me, Touch me, Affirm Me, Help Me, Gift me,
Fuck me... Spend your life with me.

Kind Is The New Bad

I thought it was cool
To be this "Boss Ass Bitch"
I thought you had to hide your heart
Vulnerability is not weakness!

A true king or queen
Is not afraid to cry or feel pain
We are humans and run on emotions
Start a new trend!

I believe our past trauma can cause a wall to be
built
I know my past has had an impact on how I handle
myself
I am finally learning how to turn that pain into re-
silience
I shouldn't have to change who I am to block the
pain others try to inflict!

I dare to start a new movement
Let's be more kind
Let's be more vulnerable
Let's not avoid human emotions!

It's cool to be kind
I am loving this new chapter in my life
It's time I finally show who I truly am
Yes, I still have some wounds and scars...

But this bloody heart is willing to still spread love,
the right people will join me on this conquest.

Different Kind Of Lovers

After round three
I thought
I didn't have
Round four in me.

Back and forth
Exchanges
Probably one of the most
Sensual experiences, I've ever had.

You are shy
It's so cute how you go about your life
Our dinner moment was nice
Thanks for showing me a good time!

Our energies matched
We were on different levels though
I may have scared you off
But wishing you the best

Thanks for one of the most sensual moments of
my life.

...

Bad boy energy
I walk in
Automatically
Eye fuck you!

Beautiful facial features
Fun energy
Gorgeous hair
You're mine tonight.

We go back to my room
Chemistry is high
Down for the ride
Switching positions is my new year's resolution.

We have great conversations
In between
Positions
You aren't just pretty, you're kind!

The next day
We hang for a bit
You leave and go about your day

I stay in bed and realize this may go nowhere in the future but...

Thanks for one of the most sexually physical moments of my life.

...

Then there's you
You were there the whole time
In front of my eyes
We never got to play.

So kind
Tried to make you mine
I had these other guys with me
But, you weren't phased.

Our conversations
Were as satisfying
As sex
Who knew, being mind fucked was fun?!

I was able to kiss those lips
Such pure energy
Rushed
Through my body!

You fed my soul
Just from the first sight

Looking into your eyes
I was able to read your mind.

You're another empath
You got me
From the first conversation
I knew this would become a kinetic relationship.

We had a cute date
I am excited for our next one
You make me feel warm inside
Just from your texts.

Thanks for making my heart, body, soul and mind
feel so alive and recognized...

Sparks

Single
No longer walking on eggshells
Damn
You were restraining me.

Gotta be picky on my dating choices
Fuck a hot body
I want a beautiful heart
With a banging soul.

A spark with a human
Is so empowering and motivating
You can feel on cloud nine
But don't be fooled by this trap.

Sparks come and go
But to fulfill my soul
I've learned the power of intuition
I know who is going to be on my mission.

A Neon Heart

I don't know when my next love will be
I do have hope that one day
I will find
Love...

Maybe, The kind of love
That I am looking for
Isn't suitable for me.

I have gotten to a point
Of trusting myself
Tuning into my intuition
Really enjoying who I am.

Getting to know yourself
Is so powerful
I have finally filled my void...

I was looking for love in the wrong places
Thinking every Mr. Wrong was Mr. Right
Blinded by pink strobe lights

I finally decided to unplug my neon heart.

This Feels Right

My connection with you
I can't describe
People say we are moving too fast
But you and I both know, this feels right!

Sometimes, a quick spark
Can fizzle out
But we are breaking history.

We have the longest world record
Of keeping a spark alive
Just one touch, from you
Sends volts of kinetic energy throughout my spine.

Like metaphysical stones
You enhance my energy
You help me see clearer
You are my Sodalite.

We say
"Fuck You"

To the critics
We know what is right.

No need for words
We just feel
We just are
We know that...

This feels right!

I Want You

You are so tempting tonight
Eye contact making me melt
Can I use you as a mop for my leak?

I know the reality of this situation
This is either going to work or not
This could be amazing but it's up to you
If you're ready to be emotionally available.

I know I am ready and willing
But in reality
A lot of people are scared of commitment.

I want you
But babe the thing is
You have to want me too!

I am a living soul
I don't fuck with ghosting
You know I want you, so the question that remains
is...

Do you want me?

4

Earth (Our Mothering Planet)

Mother Nature
Life can spiral like a tornado
It could be joyful like a midsummer day
But also dreadful like a snowstorm.

Earth has been around for over 4 billion years
It has seen so many lifetimes
So many revolutions
Different generations have come and gone.

What impact will you leave on Earth?
This planet has so much knowledge and power

Learn from it!
As I sit down with my stones and eyes closed.

Earth is whispering something to me
The message is so clear but in life we get so dis-
tracted
There is a law of attraction on this planet, in this uni-
verse!
To make the world go round, spread kindness!

Earth wouldn't be burning
If we listened to each other
This planet is our home
Treat it kindly!

It costs nothing to be kind to someone
Earth has so many dimensions to it
Weather fascinates me
We have water, land, lava, humans, animals, stars, the
Moon, the Sun, air!

Go outside
Breathe in the air this planet is providing
Thank your home planet
For the beauty it has brought upon us.

Earth, I know you have seen me in many different
lifeforms.

I promise with this life, I will help make a difference and leave a legacy that will forever benefit other humans sharing this planet with me <3.

Universe

Up in the sky
Just closing my eyes
I feel so empowered
I want this moment to be forever mine.

Standing in the dark
Waves are crashing
I see a shooting star
The stars are waving at me.

Glitter in the sand
Earth calms me so much
I feel like I belong for once
Who knew mother nature would be so motherly.

The wind keeps sending me affirming hugs
My body feels calm
All of my chakras are aligned
Is this what makes my higher consciousness ap-
pear?

I am starting to listen to you, universe
I can tell when you give me a sign
These gut feelings are becoming more and more
real
Everyday is a lesson.

Thank you for your blessings
I am here on a mission
Providing me with higher consciousness power
I am starting to become the human you knew I
would always become!

Marilyn

A woman that was ahead of her time
The world ate you up and spat you out after tasting
you
Such a talented actor
A bombshell that wasn't afraid to love.

Your vulnerability inspires me daily
Society saw you only as an image
It took death for them to realize
You were a blissful soul living her purpose!

Little do people know
You stood up for what was right
You had no problem making your own production
company
You knew your worth!

A woman that just wanted to be kind and spread
love
While living through her art
Was used and mistaken for not being smart

Oh, if they only knew the power you held.

Till today, you are one of the most talked about
souls
You inspire generations
You were never afraid to be yourself
You were never afraid to love and love hard!

The world may have failed you
But know that you have inspired me to create art,
love hard, and remember my worth in this crazy in-
dustry!

Inner Child

I believe that we sometimes forget the fun in life
When things get tough
We lose the joy in what we are doing
But when we were kids, wasn't it amazing to feel
joy?

Why does getting older have to become such a
drag?
It's ok to let your inner child come out and play
We are animals at the end of the day
Let loose and play, we are meant to play for the
sake of playing!

I look at 4 year old Antonio
He just wanted to watch TV, play with action fig-
ures and ride a swing in the park
I look at that little boy and just smile
Such happiness and ease of life reminds me to keep
going forward.

We can learn a lot from our inner child

Take a look back at who you were when you were 4
What was so joyful and easy to you?
What did you want to be or do when you grew up?
Are you fulfilling your childhood dreams?

Thank you younger Antonio for showing me that
it's ok to not be productive 24/7, go outside and enjoy
Earth with every second of life!

5

The Moon (Emotions & Instincts)

I haven't lost faith
I found new hope
As I look up to you
On this beautiful, starry night.

You give me energy
Cleansing my crystals and soul
Like a werewolf during a full moon
I am ready to scream and transform into my higher self.

Craters may be imperfections

But those are the obstacles you have to fight
To become your better self
Like all your phases...

I am ready for my next one...

A Breakup

I was hurting
Were you gas lighting?
I was confused
Did you abuse?

These emotions suck
I was in my feels for weeks
I felt like it would never go away
Love hurts!

But one day
I woke up
Realizing my truth and growth
This relationship didn't serve me.

Why was I forcing something that wasn't meant to
be?
Was I trying to save you?
I know I like to heal
Do I need healing?

I spent months working on my inner demons
I thought my savior complex was finished
But dating you made me realize
I had one last battle with it.

I am taking this experience as a positive
I still love the person you are
I just think we both need emotional growth
I am on a beautiful journey of discovering myself.

Thanks for serving your purpose
Even if you don't see my side to life
Just know I wish nothing but love for you
But now, it's time for this butterfly to fly.

Feel It Out

I can't fully dive in
I don't think it's commitment issues
I believe in guarding my heart
It's too sensitive to be played with.

I want to make sure
The next person to hold it
Treats it with kindness
I deserve genuine love.

Before we dive in
I need a life jacket
Incase we plunge too deep
I need to make sure I can float away.

I feel things out
I use to not think
I would move way too fast
It was a vicious dating cycle.

I learned my lessons

If you are cool with this
Let's feel it out and
See if our vibe is right.

First Dates

I am so nervous
Can I put my heart at risk again?
I am so easily hurt
Is potential love worth the risk?

The butterflies of getting a text from someone new
The hype of getting dressed for a fun night
planned
I am always vulnerable
But being vulnerable in front of a crush is its own
kind of monster.

My cheeks are red when thinking about all the po-
tential scenarios
I have to shut off this anxiety whether its good or
bad
As I am on my way to this date
I just have to remember, at the end of the day...

No matter where this leads to

I have had a lot of practice with liking someone and
things going south
As a vulnerable, sensitive human
I am ready to try love again...

This will always be an anxiety trigger for me
I have learned how to love with a wounded heart
I am done thinking a man can stitch my heart back
up
I am the one that will cherish it.

During first dates
The thrill overtakes my body
Sometimes I can't think or see straight
But I trust that my heart will be ok.

Through all the trials and tribulations, I know this
wounded heart is a love warrior!

I Feel FEELINGS

I feel a lot
My mood changes
Like the weather
I go from joyful to gloomy.

Yes, I am an empath
Honestly I didn't realize this
Till my late twenties
Life now makes sense.

I always thought I was crazy
I never felt like I fit in
I was so sensitive in school
It made my bullies, bully me more.

It's funny how people
Will project their insecurities
On someone sensitive and vulnerable
Then when you react, you are gaslighted as to why
you are being so sensitive and crazy.

Looking back at my life
I understand so much now
I am special
My mirror neurons are beautiful.

I help people
But now I know
If I am manipulated and drained
I can't help anymore.

I can't save you
I can be a part of your journey as a friend
But using my empath power
Is not going to work.

I always thought it was a bad thing
That I had so many emotions
Society made me think
That being vulnerable showed weakness.

Courage comes from vulnerability
My emotions guide me through life
I am proud to be sensitive
I will not live by your narrative anymore.

.

Built Up Tension

Driving me around
You got me in my feels
You go out of your way
Just to understand me.

Age is just a number
Your awareness
At your age
Is beautiful.

You don't want me to leave
I wish I could extend my stay
Just sitting next to you
Is so magical.

It's funny
How I never had a partner
Make me feel
The way you make me feel.

I never have luck

In New York
Why are the good ones
Always living outside of my state?

All of my theories
Are starting to come
True
I now know what intuitive love is.

Even if it's for a moment
I will always remember that jolt in my body
You fed my soul so hard
I can't wait for the next moment...

When our auras can lay together, and we can re-
lease our built up tension.

Rome

Bike rides late at night
There's a hint of a romantic spark
A little mystery of who you are
Is making me want to know more.

Like the Pantheon
I am the light that shines for you
Rome wasn't built in a day
I understand I am going to need a few months to let
you see that there is more to do with me.

Nights with you
When my body
Is your Roman feast
Devour me with every lick.

This connection is unexplainable
I have become the Cleopatra to your Julius Caesar
Entering your job out of nowhere
We may have changed each other's lives.

Organic connections is what I yearn for
Eye contact and attention is what I push for
Like the Colosseum
Are we fighting against this connection?

I will be the gladiator to your heart cage
Fighting for what feels right
I just want to kiss you
Under the Roman moonlight.

6

Mars (Sex & Action)

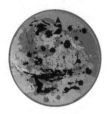

Embody me
Let me enter your UFO
My presence is strong
My Mars is in Scorpio.

My need for love and lust
Can conflict on many levels
All I am asking, is for you to
Phone my home.

I know my flaws
I usually like to get my own way
But on my journey to Saturn
I am learning that not everything has to go my way.

I do have highs and lows
Like the terrain on Mars
Everyday is a new lesson
Maybe my attachment to the universe is making me
disinterested in Earthly men.

It's time to live an extraterrestrial life.

Vibezzz

It's summer
And I'm in heat
My body is on fire
Can you cool me down?

I like your energy
You make me feel safe
Rosè on tap
But you can be my bottle of choice.

Hey, we may not talk after this weekend
But the energy that you are feeding my soul with
Has me feeling so rejuvenated and not used
Why don't we play fairytale boyfriends for this
weekend?

Vibezzz
Buzzing
Chilling
Licking my feelings.

Touching
Lunching
Biting
You know I'm not fighting.

Impress
Release my stress
Make me catch
My breath.

Using My Imagination

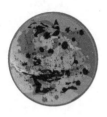

This ride in the universe
Can get a little lonely
I use to watch things on the computer to help me
But it's time to use my imagination.

I turn to myself
For pleasure
Why have an incubus try to satisfy me?
I trust my sexual energy
I play the best when alone!

It's beautiful when you can rely on yourself for a
release
Built up tension can hinder thoughts
When I think with my other head
That's when troubled men come my way...

Now that I trust myself fully
I have no problem wrapping my vulnerable self

All in my bed alone
My imagination and hand can create the best or-
gasm, I have ever experienced!

My Body Like Wine

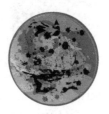

I want it
I may have won it
Do you want it?
The thirst for what I got.

Shit feels good
This is raw energy right here
We vibe to the fullest
Crystallize this moment.

Come take a sip of what I got
We don't have to be cuffed
My soul is satisfied
Don't worry, this time I won't be attached!

Come
Take a seat
Let me hold you
While, you take a sip of what I'm about.

Body Heat

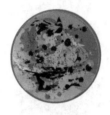

Tonight I am feeling sexy
My pink lips
Size 32" Waist
With a thick cake that's waiting to be tasted.

Papi
Let me show you
What this Italian, Dominican
Is all about.

Tonight's mood is
Non committal
For once
I just want a hot sexual encounter.

Whining my body on the dance floor
Your eyes are mesmerized
As I wave for you to join me
I am warming up my oven.

Sexy energy and my hands on your hips

This music is hot
And so is my body
Why don't I take you back and show you...

How I can warm you up with this body heat.

Attention

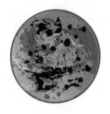

I see you
I want it
Can you
Give me it?

Oh, put that away
I am not talking
About body parts...
I want ATTENTION!

See
Human validation
Is essential
To every human.

If 2020
Taught us anything
It's that, a humans touch or affirmation
Can make us feel so important.

Even if it's for one night only

Make me feel like
Your ruler of the night
I want to be your strobe light.

Maybe it's a little vain
Wanting to feel needed
Maybe it's humanistic
To desire this attention.

I have had moments
Of seeking validation in the wrong areas
I am suddenly wondering
If attention, I really am seeking...

Is it from myself?

Being Positive Isn't Being A Bitch

I am a positive person
But you think
I am being a
Bitch...

You think
Me avoiding
Gossip
Is boring.

Just because
I focus on good energy
Does not mean
I am fake.

I have learned

That I don't care
For your complains
Anymore.

If this is true friendship
Then we shouldn't be based
On agony and other people's business
We should be encouraging and developing as hu-
mans.

Inspire to be
The best people
That we can be
That is friendship.

My home base is positivity
If that is being a bitch
Then
I am the biggest bitch...

You will ever meet <3.

Mr. Nana

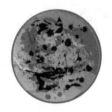

Time to drop the facade
This acting game is getting old
I am so tired from hiding
I am letting down my steel wall!

Nana was the strength I needed
I was so scared of my heart being hurt
I shielded my vulnerability with a glass wall
My confidence made it look like it was steel
Little did people know, I can shatter in seconds...

As I have gotten older
I really started getting into my own groove
It's sexy to be vulnerable
Vulnerability is my new shield
I have no problem laying it all out there.

Nana served his purpose
He taught me about strength
He taught me to not take anyone's crap

He taught me to stand up for what I believe in
But as much confidence he gave me, he was wearing a mask, because Antonio was hiding behind him scared.

I have found the courage to move on and to be Antonio 24/7! I look back at all my "Nana" moments and say thank you, but it's time for this bird to fly.

Fun Times

My memories are so blurry
All I know, was that, last night was fun
One too many drinks
But I regret nothing.

Locking lips with a few people
No strings attached
I want to play tonight
Feels so good to not have my heart played with.

When I walk into a situation
Knowing that my heart is secured
I get to let loose
Let my wild side out.

I don't need to call this side Nana anymore
This is a part of Antonio as well
I don't have to be serious or emotional all the time
I am human and am allowed to have a wild side.

Let loose and let your inner child play!

7

Jupiter (Abundance & Growth)

Like the Roman God
I want to rule your heaven
I find success through family with my Jupiter in
Virgo
Why is it hard to build something with you?

I have a strong sense of spirituality
Not displayed in philosophy
Jupiter being the social planet
Can I enter your circle?

Like Jupiter

My heart is massive
The red spot in it, is from the arrow of love you shot
Instead of hitting me with love, it pierced me
My heartbeat is as fast as Jupiter's rotation
These feelings and aching heart has me stuck in a
love storm.

Jupiter, I ask that you show me strength and bring
back my beliefs.
Seems like I lost my way while trying to find you
You help me with my optimism and creativity
I tried to be a ruler of someone's heaven and all that
left me was with...

A damaged heart.

Timelines

I do have hope for you
You are a good person
Just distracted by life
I think you are going to start to learn about your
emotional intelligence.

I have a feeling
Our time isn't over yet
I am not talking about anytime soon
But maybe a few years down the line.

I think it was the right people
At the wrong time
I do believe in a parallel universe
Maybe we are dating in a different galaxy.

Whether it's this life
Or the next life
We will be reunited
In some type of way.

Until then
Take care
You have a heart of gold
That leaks blood because of your wounds.

Just remember I understand your intentions and
also your distractions!

Manifestation

I look up to the sky
Asking the universe
When will my dreams come true?
I think it's time I manifest them.

This idea
May seem foreign
But I believe
We attract what we give.

I want to do good in this world
I want to work on myself
I want to keep on learning about cultures and life
I want to learn about myself!

I am still growing on this journey
With this divine power
That cosmic touch
I believe I have the power to create what I want.

I manifest
A prosperous life
A beautiful career
Mental health strength
Good and fulfilling relationships...

What do you manifest?

What I Want

I want to work with good people
I want to be surrounded by positive influences
I want a lot of alone time
I want to be in my own bed.

I want real people
I want deep conversations
I want shared vulnerability
I want more meditation!

I want a magical artist career
I want good relationships
I want sustainable mental health
I want to own my power of empathy!

I want to spread love
I want to create
I want to write more
I want to be forever happy!

Good People + Good Energy

I don't know how to describe
This feeling
It's time to write about
Something new!

This past week
Has been one of the most rejuvenating
Times in my life
I never knew, I needed so much!

I am addicted to good connections
People that feed my energy
You know, for once
I met all the good people!

I've been through some
Ups and downs
I've had narcissist and bad people
Use me.

Every week
I am learning
Something new
I am learning how I have been played the whole
time.

I am learning the power of manifestation
I am starting to put my concentration
Into beautiful things
Law of attraction!

I attracted so many amazing people
It's so beautiful
To see what can happen in your life
When you spread love and kindness.

Writing this now
I am tearing up
Because, I haven't had my soul touched like this
in...
The universe knows how long!

Thank you universe, for always sending me signs
when I need them.
The power of manifestation and law of attraction is
one of the most amazing discoveries I have found.

True Friends

They say when you get older
Your clique gets smaller
Quality over
Quantity.

I will take a wine night with five friends
Over
A club with
Twenty social climbers.

I am now seeing who I can trust
I am now realizing who stabbed me in the back
Like a book with an attractive cover,
What's inside is so much better.

Deeper conversations
A safe environment
These are the people
That I want in my life.

I am lucky to finally see who the real ones are
It feels good to finally see which friends were there
this whole time
It's funny, with less friends
I have more emotional support.

To my friends that are my soulmates
Cheers to you for inspiring me
Thank you for always having my heart at interest
It's beautiful to realize soulmates aren't just people
you date...

They are the friends that will put your soul first
and love you no matter what!

I Trust Me

For once
I am listening to myself
This thrill is crazy
Is this what it means to love myself?

I am starting to trust myself
I am starting to feel intuition
I can see clearly again.

You know
If I was blind like a bat
I would still understand what was going on
My intuition power has increased.

I had a wild year
Learned some lessons
Lost some friends
Manifested some real shit!

I am starting to understand who

Antonio is
He's always been here
My higher consciousness knew it the whole time.

I am beyond happy
That I finally learned
The meaning of a "gut" feeling
I finally learned to trust myself.

I look into my reflection and can finally say... I
TRUST YOU!

Moving On

Maybe, I am not over you
Maybe, I never will be
I still love you
But, it's time I move on.

I can look back
Remember the times we had
I can remember the lessons I learned
But, it's time I move on.

I am about to start my new life
This transition is so empowering
My heart still aches for you
But, it's time I move on.

I wish you well
I hope you can make someone really happy
You deserve happiness
But, it's time I move on.

Meeting new people
Feeling new vibes
Sometimes I compare them to you
But, it's time I move on.

Thank you for everything
I want you to know that I will be there in the future
I need to take this journey and next chapter alone
I am moving on.

See you in a different life ...

Success

What defines your success?
I used to think that if I had millions of dollars
I would be so happy
I guess growing up poor, that's all I could think of...

Money
Fame
A lot of different "goals"
Can distract us to what we really want.

To be honest
I wanted to be an artist
Just to live a fun and rich lifestyle
How couldn't I see that my art was more impor-
tant?

Social media can be dangerous
We start comparing ourselves
We start changing our goals

We start seeing worth in how many followers we
have.

I finally broke out of that vicious cycle
I'd rather be a struggling artist
Using my art as therapy for people and myself
Than to sell out on who I truly am for money and
fame.

I rather be my own boss
Than work a 9-5
I want to love what I do
Not do what I do to make good money.

Fame can come with the territory
You just have to remain humble
Remember your roots
Remember why you are on this earth.

I live to inspire
I hope my art helps people
And for me, that
Is success!

8

Saturn (Ambition & Discipline)

It's my time to shine
Damn turning 29 feels so new
I don't know the person I was a year ago
Hell, a few months ago I was thinking differently.

Am I finally an adult?
What is an adult according to society?
Age may give you experience
But you can still be any age and not have personal or
emotional growth!

Emotional intelligence is important
I am on a mental health journey
I am on a empath journey
I finally know who the fuck I am!

Excuse my french
But feeling THIS ALIVE IS AMAZING
I think I know what bliss feels like
The satisfaction of life I have on the inside is unex-
plainable.

Yes, I feel a lot of emotions
I take on people's pain
I have an anxiety disorder
But I am a good fucking human.

I am learning
I am living
This journey is opening so many different doors for
me
Intuition is finally speaking to me.

With my obstacles
I am finally learning
How to not fully suffer from them
But be the best human I can be.

I went through a hell of a year
Hell, life is a never ending rollercoaster
I went too high
I'm in space.

As I drive on my 29th lap
On the rings of Saturn

I am starting to see my life come into fruition
Manifestation at its finest.

Saturn show me
The divinity of life
My mission for the greater good
And the all seeing eye to protect my learning soul.

Me, Myself & I

I look in the mirror
I am finally happy with my reflection
A smile starts to form
From knowing, I've made it.

I please myself in so many ways
Not just with my hand
But with my mind and soul
Writing love letters to the universe
I finally feel so free.

This can be a long journey
Driving on the rings of Saturn
But I have the best company with me...

Me, Myself & I.

29.5 Chances

I gave you 29.5 chances
You gave me 1
I gave you 29.5 reasons as to why I am amazing
You gave me none.

It takes Saturn 29.5 years to revolve around the sun
I am 29.5 years of age
I am on my mission to this new destination
You're lucky I even gave you a .5 chance.

The reason I stopped at 29.5 and not 30 you ask?
I finally realized
You weren't even worth being in my life
When I hit that number.

I am done being walked over
Manipulated
My good heart
Gets tossed around with you a lot.

I wish you healing and growth
But I am currently on Saturn

I'm about to complete my 360
Damn who knew a half a year I saved for myself
was worth so much.

I am keeping that .5 to myself
For when I reach level 30
I will have a better idea of who I am
Without people that blind my sight in life.

Codependency

I love you so much
I see me in you
We coexist, but the problem is
We are codependent.

This word always scared me
How could I lose my identity by being around
someone?
I was starting to become the "fixer"
In this relationship.

Now codependency can be 50/50
I let your energy affect me in such a toxic way
Anyone that knows me knows that I never bite my
tongue
Seems like a cat caught my tongue when I'm with
you.

For a few years I was blinded by the flashy things
we experienced
This poor guy from Long Island
Getting to explore Treasure Island

I thought I hit a gold mine, but really I'm on a land-mine.

A great person
A damaged soul
Two friends that need some time
To learn who they are and then maybe...

We can meet again.

Boundaries

I now know what the fine line is
It's transparent
But has a force behind it, it's called a
Boundary.

I use to think that letting people know
That I wont engage with their toxic behavior
Would come off rude.

I finally realized that
It's ok to let someone know
What your boundaries are
I refuse to be in a toxic environment now.

Talks with my therapist
Has me seeing better than ever
I now know...
What Antonio wants!

I have no problem
Stating what makes me feel uncomfortable

I refuse to lose myself in order to not wreck the ship!
Me letting you know how I feel shouldn't cause a tsunami in your brain!

Open communication is key
Instead of living in a whirlpool of dread
Grab that life jacket and know that
Your boundaries are what will keep you afloat.

Expectations

I use to expect a lot from people
I have learned that
People let you down
More than they help you!

Having less expectations
Can lead to more surprises
When another human actually
Steps up to the plate!

There is only a few things I expect from people
now
They must respect who I am
Spread love and not hate
Respect my boundaries...

The rest is up to them to truly show me if they
have what it takes to share the same realm as me.

Time For Change

I think I need a break from you New York
Not a goodbye
But a see you later
I see new opportunities on the horizon.

I have spent my whole life here
This city helped shape me
I have learned who I am
I can see it clearly now.

With this new version of me
Well, really the old me that came to light
I am ready to start a new chapter
In a new city with new people.

I am tapping into other creative pursuits
I am excited for this new journey
I was nervous of change for awhile
But I know that the universe has my back!

It's time to take all my knowledge about myself
and live my truth in a new environment!

RIP To Tony

As I approach 30
10.20 has never looked so much brighter than now
My grandpa died on 10.20
Antonio was born on 10.20.

This number comes to me a lot
An angel looking down
A reminder to keep on going
A sign for Antonio being reborn!

Tony was a cute nickname given to me
But I have always been Antonio
A legacy created for me
It's time as an adult to lead my own path!

Tony
Was this young and innocent human
With such a vulnerable heart
So easy to crack.

He was scared a lot
Super social but very introverted
He went through a lot of phases to find himself

Created different images of his "best self".

I look back at those years
Beautiful lessons
Heartbreaking moments
A lot of laughs
With a lot of tears.

As I create this new journey
Getting ready for my Saturn Return
I want to say, thank you Tony
For showing me that it's ok to cry and it's ok to laugh.
Be weird, be funny, be quirky, own who you are!

If I could go back in time and tell my younger self something, I would say,

"You are a star, always be you and don't be afraid to love and feel all those beautiful emotions you feel, you're so fucking special".

9

Uranus (Rebellion & Reformation)

A planet of revolution
The butt of every joke
With Uranus in Taurus
It's time to show some innovative energy.

I am starting to change my views on
Who I let in my circle and
How I spend my money
It's time to manifest a new life.

A revolution is needed for me
It's time to lead my own way

Time to stop conforming to what society says
Life is all about perception, time to put on new con-
tact lenses.

Perception

Maybe its a change of attitude
I am seeing life so differently lately
My anxiety is at an all time low
Life is all about perception, right?

Everything that happens to you
You have a few ways to react
Nowadays we RESPOND
You can choose to let the circumstance own you or
to feel it and grow.

I have had my fair share
Of battles
If you only knew
How reactive I used to be.

I have learned to trust the universe
I can't control everything
Being a passenger isn't so bad

Don't get me wrong, I still wear my seat belt be-
cause I am my own security!

I have always been an optimist
My anxiety and ego lead me to a road of doubt
Now that I have clear vision again
I am driving this fine ass car on the rings of Sat-
urn...

Someone else's perception can deceive you.
Listen to your intuition
Feel for what's right and...
Reach for the stars baby!

Liberated

People aren't use to this new attitude
I honestly love where I am in life
I have no problem stating my opinion
Free to be.

People will judge when they see someone living
their best life
Their bodies are projectors
They have no problem projecting their own fear of
liberation on you
While they project their moody light on you
Use it for your self-love catwalk that they will
never forget!

This high is amazing
I am free, I feel like me and that's all I need
Live your truth
Shame resilience is my trait
Who is joining me on this runway towards libera-
tion?

Energy Vampires

OMG, I finally know who you are
See, I always thought you loved Halloween
You were dressed up as a vampire
This whole time during our friendship.

I guess you do come alive at night
Waiting for a vulnerable moment
In your friends apartment
Dumping all of your baggage and lies.

So you don't like drinking blood?
I think I figured how you stay so "young"
Like some witches
You suck the energy out of people.

Your words
Are your fangs
Your toxic behavior
Is your cape.

Me being nice wasn't my weakness
Yes, it was my vulnerability
But now I know
I don't need a stake to get rid of you.

My vulnerability and intuition
Are beautiful things in the world
Holy water and a cross isn't going to work
You know what will?

Killing you with kindness
Now that your fangs don't scare me anymore
Now that I can see that your cape is an invisible
shield
I am moving on with my life.

I am done giving you good energy to devour!

Eggshells

I felt so controlled
One little word
I was yelled at
Was this becoming an emotionally abusive relation-
ship?

You know walking on eggshells
I am most likely going to crack each one
I am too liberated as a human
To be nervous to speak my mind.

Gaslighted
To make it seem like I was the crazy one
I think you got it wrong
Just because I am on a road to enlightenment
doesn't give you the right to project.

Everyone has baggage
But you my friend
Love to use the closest people in your life as

Your dumpster.

There's a difference between
Venting and dumping
Venting lets you blow off some steam and seek ad-
vice
Dumping is throwing your problems on someone
else.

I have no problem now
Letting go of relationships
With people that make you feel so drained
People will love to use you as a punching bag.

Vampires
See, those I like
Energy Vampires
Those, I need to avoid.

I've learned to walk on a flat ground
Hanging with you
I was slipping on yolk and cracking shells
I am finally closing that chapter of living in a mess.

Shedding Skin

Like a snake
I am shedding skin
I am finally walking away
From everything that was holding my truth back.

I feel so free
I feel like me
I am finally
Seeing what it's like to be alive.

I can't put the blame on you
I allowed you to hold me back
Maybe I wasn't ready
You were my shield at times.

This wounded person
Now has an army
Of
One!

Shedding the dead skin
Closing my final chapter
Starting a new book
Let's see where I go next...

Change

It feels weird that I am not the same person I was
yesterday
I have been orbiting in space for awhile now
Every planet I land on
Shapes me to be a different person.

So many sides to me
Every moment is a lesson
I refuse to be scared of change
From what the universe is showing me.

It's time to embrace this change, for I am now un-
derstanding my life purpose!

Bad Bitch Energy

Rolling up to the club
I am not here to please anyone
I manifested my night
Fuck popping bottles
Time to radiate this fiery aura.

Dancing in my own aura bubble
Music inspires me
Give me that
5.6.7.8.

My body speaks for itself
There may be a hundred people here
But I am only focused on
Myself.

No. I don't want to hook up
If you're going to be in my way
Can you at least, grab me a glass of
Prosecco?!

It's amazing
How once you feel yourself
You exude such dominating energy
It feels good to just live!

Being a "Bad Bitch"
Doesn't mean
To be heartless
It means
Be yourself and authentic.

I am kind
I walk to my own beat
I treat others with respect
But also don't take anyone's toxic shit.

Now that's what I call having Bad Bitch Energy.

I Want To Be Alone For Awhile

I always loved a romantic high
But for once
I think
I want to be alone.

For awhile
I always dreamed of
Prince Charming and
Falling in love.

This fairytale
Isn't short lived
I still have work to do
To slay my dragon.

I'm learning
That
I don't need...

Saving.

I am tired
Of thinking
That every guy
I meet.

Could be the one
It's time for me
To understand
That I am the one!

10

Neptune (Intuition & Imagination)

This journey has been such an adventure
As I reach the end of it
I pass by Neptune
So blue like my home's ocean.

A generational planet
A ruler of dreams, imagination and the unconscious
I find inspiration through ambition and hard work
This journey has been a hard lesson.

I am returning to earth soon

As a new human
As Antonio!

On my way to entering a new decade
Passing you reminds me
That my brain is so powerful
I have a lust for life and use to let a lot of other peo-
ple interfere with my life mission.

God of the sea
The cosmic power I get from you
I can finally control the tsunami of anxious thoughts
I've learned how to think like a calm river.

Anxiety

Overwhelmed
I wake up in panics sometimes
Showering should be meditative
Why am I having thoughts of random scenarios
and negative outcomes?

Fear of confrontation
Adrenaline rushing through my body
From false thoughts of
A situation that is never going to happen.

What is versus What if
I need to start changing my perspective of thinking
Why do I always jump to the worst case scenario?
I have catastrophic thinking.

Family patterns do not help
Being an empath makes it worse
Toxic friends make me anxious
Who can I talk to?

Therapy
I finally found an objective voice
That is willing to listen
I can vent and start reflecting on my conversations.

This mental disorder
Will always be a constant fight
But I am starting to feel that I have the power
To not have my mental health define who I am.

Break the stigma, IT'S OK TO NOT BE OK!

The Days My Prayers Changed

I use to idolize a man
Sitting above the sky
With judgement on his fingers
In one snap, you could die.

A fearful god, they say
A pregnant virgin, they say
A son that was hung on a crucifix, they say
Men writing how we should behave in a book, they
read.

Now listen, I love a good fairytale
But these stories sound like a horror movie
I understand some humans need a person or thing
to believe in
This year I chose to give my everything to the uni-
verse.

No man is going to decide how I live
Or when I will die
I am here to be a good human and help create posi-
tive change
I believe in love and community.

I see life so differently now
We are here to help each other
When I realized that religion spreads more hate
than love
That was the day my prayers changed!

Dear, Universe
Thank you for the abundance of joy
Thank you for manifestation of a beautiful life
Thank you for love
Thank you for guiding me on this wild Saturn trip!

What I Really See

You say certain words
Why are you hiding from me?
I understand being seen
Is vulnerable.

You tell me
"I'm OK"
While I can see tears building up
Deep in your eyes.

I feel energy
I feel love
I feel a lot
I feel you!

I have a good tendency of reading what is sublimi-
nally being said
You think you're sly
My third eye is strong
And I am so connected to you!

I will always see the truth
I love your vulnerability
Just know that I am always here for you
I understand all of you!

...

Even when we drift apart, I will be connected to
you.

Drugs

I'm good.
I get overstimulated way too easily
I am tired of being under an influence
That triggers me.

My higher conscious and universe
Influence me on the regular
A natural meditative high that I can't explain
I rather choose me as my drug choice.

The anxiety feeling that happens the next day
when you wake up post high
Why be in a realm where I can't think straight?
Why swallow something that will trigger my mental
health and higher being?
I believe this is a part of my return, I am now aware
of what makes me joyful and alive!

Silver Lining

I believe in optimism
I see the silver lining in everything
The universe will give you challenges
Try to see the reason in them.

If you can grow from these challenges
You will become stronger
More connected with the universe
Start to learn who you are.

Conversations with my higher self
Understanding the silver lining
Is game changing
I am starting to make negative situations into posi-
tive circumstances!

It's funny how life alone is a silver lining...

Who Am I?

Woah
An acid trip?
I believe it's called a...
Nana trip.

Out of body experiences
I am watching myself sleep
Floating around my room
Not all ghosts are dead.

Someone is speaking into my ear
I can't make out all the words
But I know that
It feels right.

Psychic power
This is the highest high
I have ever felt
Naturally stimulating my higher consciousness.

It's almost time
To go back into my body
I found some answers
Who knew my subconscious was so fucked up.

This spiritual journey
Just started
There are some days I wake up in the middle of the
night
Startled with heavy energy hovering over me.

I use to be scared
I now accept that
These entities coming to play with me
Are starting to awaken my higher power.

I now know Who I Am!

11

Pluto (Power & Rebirth)

You ignored me
Like Pluto
Why do the smaller and more shy ones
Get pushed to the end of the line?

I always felt a connection to Pluto
The controversy of whether it was a planet or not?
A major planet turned into a dwarf planet
Reminds me of how I was always your ninth choice.

Just like Pluto
I deserve love

Being the underdog of this Solar System
We are fighters and won't be dismissed.

You could've been
The Charon to my Pluto
But you chose to be
The Titan to his Saturn.

But like Pluto
You may think of me as the farthest and coldest
thing
Existing in your Solar System
I still have a lot to learn but I am currently the best
version of myself.

I live for the underdog story
I blast through these obstacles the universe gives me
Pluto you remind me
That Antonio was always there, I take all these life
lessons in stride!

It's time to awake my higher consciousness and show
the universe what Antonio embodies as a loving human!

Doing Me

I am holding my own hand
I have been through a lot of shit
I am almost three decades old
But I feel like I have lived for centuries.

The things you endure
Can make you strong or weak
I have chosen to not make these obstacles my ene-
mies
But to embrace them.

Being single
Doesn't mean I am alone
I feel the most alive currently
It feels good to just..."Do Me".

So cliche
This simple saying
But it's one of the hardest actions

To actually do in life.

What is "Doing Me"?
This meaning is different per person
For me, it means not relying on a man
It means, walking to my own beat of the drum.

I always was a leader
I refuse to find validation in a person
My validation comes from
The things I do to be a good creative human in this
universe.

Some people want to harm and spread hate
I take the lighter road
I believe in spreading love
With every single breath I have...

I will always DO ME.

A Shooting Star

As I look into the sky
I saw a shooting star and made a wish
I wished for a love so big with a partner
That my whole universe would feel centered...

But the universe reminded me that the biggest rela-
tionship I need to conquer is a relationship with my-
self.

Self Advice

I choose who to give my energy to
I am selective with my time
There are a lot of people
That will suck your soul dry.

Be aware
Listen to yourself
For every good person you meet
There will be a mean person waiting.

Follow your own lead
Don't be afraid to do you own thing
You are making the Milky Way your highway
Driving on realizations and cosmic energy.

This isn't a collision course
This is a higher conscious conversation
Forget a road trip
This is universal

Blast off to the unknown.

Trust me, the universe has your back!

Old Antonio

You always been there
It's been a crazy journey
But you have been there all along
I was blinded by fake, flashing lights.

Seeking validation
Through the wrong temptation
I was always trying to find myself
But all along, you were by my side.

I said bye to Tony and Nana
I am saying hello to Antonio
That four year old that just wanted to perform
The mama's boy that never wanted to leave the
house
The kid that was bullied his whole life.

I went through a lot of traumatic shit growing up
This has been the most healing time in my life

I always hated being sensitive
I hated myself for a long time.
As I welcome you back to my life, I am sorry I lost
you, I lost who I was for 29 years.

I feel alive again
I feel love again
I feel like me for the first time
I can see clearly now!

I am done hiding
This new journey just started and I am so ready
for...
Antonio's Return!

I Found Myself

It's wild
I was lost in space for so long
Trying on different versions of myself
I finally found the version that fits.

A rocket blasting off
A man's first step on the Moon
No gravity
I am free!

**Free to me is knowing that I finally found myself.
I am no longer lost!**

Antonio Liranzo is a performer and writer from New York. He grew up in Long Island and moved to the city to follow his artistic pursuits. Writing poetry has been a passion since he was a child and has always dreamed of having his work published so he may share his passion with the public. As a mental health advocate, poetry has also become a source of therapy. Sharing these life stories in a poetic form with a little help and inspiration from pop culture, it's Antonio's mission to share in hopes that his words can be related to and be just as therapeutic to his readers. Be sure to check out his previous work, *Falling Angel: Rising Phoenix (2020) and Romance In A Modern World (2021)*. Thank you for your continuous support. Go out there and love freely and fiercely!

Instagram: @AntonioILiranzo
Twitter: @AntonioILiranzo

CPSIA information can be obtained
at www.ICGtesting.com
Printed in the USA
LVHW020726300421
686058LV00012B/854